The Struggle

Writings by

Dennis M. Stanfield

Marc
Man
Arts

DEN
POET

2

Copyright Page

ISBN: 987-0-615-97859-8

Publication Date: February 2014
Release Date: July 2014

Book Design by Dennis M. Stanfield
Book Cover Design by Michele Crawford

For more information and other books please visit the websites below or email the author directly.

dennis_stanfield@yahoo.com

www.dennismarc.webs.com

www.denpoet.wordpress.com

3

Letter from my sister…

To Marc:

You've been through a lot

It's been a long time coming

But you haven't given up

And the result is stunning

I just want to say that I'm proud

I am a proud sister

I am proud that you have stuck it out and finished

I am impatient at times and so are you

But you always say patience is a virtue and it holds to be true

All I ever want is for you to be happy and live with no regrets too

Be proud of who you are and know that no one will take that away from you

Your opportunities are endless so you'll be on your way soon

I'm excited for this next chapter in your life and the things that will ensue

I am a proud sister

Dedication

This book is dedicated to the strugglers; to their personal struggle and the struggles of anyone they carry. The struggle of single mothers and fathers, kids of separated parents, siblings raising siblings, first generation college kids, that guy on the corner, and the falsely accused. The struggle of dreamers, lovers, fighters, those with broken hearts, those with pain, and those discriminated against. Through your struggle be an inspiration and never give in. You're not struggling alone.

Introduction

The Struggle

This is the struggle
The rising from underneath rubble
The pain and the stress
The fear and doubt not being at your best
Although it can be difficult it can be beautiful
To get past you have to embrace no matter how unusual
See, you can't let struggle win
You must always maintain a grin
No one said this thing called life would be a cake walk
You speak doubt and it'll become real talk
Everyone goes through moments of struggle
Sorry to bust your bubble
But how you handle the struggle will take you far in life
You'll never have a chance if you don't roll the dice
Flowers grow in the rain and after the rain comes the sun
Welcome to the struggle…

Table of Contents

7

The Struggle:

Through the Eyes of My Heart

"It's better to write for yourself and have no public, than to write for the public and have no self." – Cryeil Connolly

The Struggle – My Struggle

I've made some bad choices in my life
God has tried to show me, but I ignored the light
I lead myself into darkness I confess
The devil is a lie, but I could've said no
I had the power to say no
Thinking I'm strong when I'm really weak
Hiding my insecurity through lies and deceit
I'm really weak
The world is so easy to fall in love with
And hard to let go
It puts on an enticing show
Lord, I've heard Your call and responded, "later"
Well now is later
I can't afford to ignore anymore
I can't put it off anymore
I'm all ears
Releasing my fears
Placing all my problems in Your hands
Throwing away mine and accepting Your plans
I have to learn to get out my own way
I want to give my girl the best
My quest
My struggle

The Struggle – Miles Davis Kind of Blue

I could see the storm approaching with a rush
So I went for the umbrella to protect us
But sometimes you can't stop the rain
She seemed like a vampire with fangs
Talking about she could change me
She could save me
I prepared her by saying no long term
The further we go the faster the bridge burns
Didn't faze her
Confident in her ways
To no avail
Now what was good isn't good
And my flaws are brought forth from under the hood
As I slowly rise
The demons laugh at my inability to compromise

I could see the storm approaching with a rush
So I went for the umbrella to protect us
But sometimes you can't stop the rain
Maybe it's my fault. I should've given her the umbrella alone to stop any raining pain
And that there gives me the blues
Premeditated murder to something that hasn't had a chance
There's only been a glance
In the chance of life and what it holds
Who am I to keep it away at the distance of a pole?
What I'm not looking for keeps finding me
And it never is to be
Attachments get attached like an email file
But gets returned with an unable to send and a cryptic smile
As a man there's no forgiveness to my own pain, but I hope they understand
I'll continue to drown my blues through this pain pen in my hand

11

The Struggle – Clearing My Mind

This may seem like rhymes on paper lines
But this is just me clearing out my mind
Going into the attic and clearing some space
But each item cleared is not going to waste

11-30-04, eight years to the day
I was feeling an empty kind of way
The pain of loss has been my nemesis
Something I didn't realize was so serious
An emptiness I didn't want filled
And if it was going that way I ran out on the bill
Sounds like an excuse running through my thoughts
The choice of payment is mine
Not looking to confront what haunts me
Though it confronts me
…one day

This may seem like rhymes on paper lines
But this is just me clearing out my mind
Going into the attic and clearing some space
But each item cleared is not going to waste
(Continued)

Baby I like you but I'm not there yet
That place where actual feelings are kept
That place where your feelings are kept
My feelings are fish, catch and release
Not sure I could sit still in bed peace
This life is full of choices
And voices
Telling you how to live
But the advice usually comes back to benefit them
And not you
Shoveling the snow creating my own path with my own design
If that differs from your thought process, fine
I'm going at a steady enough pace for myself
In no rush to climb the shelf
I hate to disappoint but I'm not ready to fall, its bad for my health
I'm clearing my mind, never mine me
Like workers striking on coal mining

This may seem like rhymes on paper lines
I'm just clearing my mind

13

The Struggle – For the Time Being

Wake up and my eyes dash to your silhouette
You're not really there, but in my mind is where you're kept
Because I only have eyes for you
I see a stunning young lady but comparisons amount to you
She's not you because God only made one, not two
It's like a spell that consumes my thoughts
And it's been a while
I've missed that smile
They say you never miss it till it's gone
Well I miss the other half of my throne
The warmth of that smile on my face
Hugs with my hands around your waist
I know I messed up and pushed you away
I want nothing more than to have your sun shine back my way
But for the time being I'll stare at our photos framed
That giant smile of yours untamed
I'm in a caged depression, for the time being

The Struggle – How I Lost My Lady

Still eats me when it crosses my mind
The potential of us…

Who ever thought you'd get burnt by telling the truth
Her girls in her ear altering the story like a spoof
We started hanging by the lockers
Back in the times of the Cleveland Rockers
Pretty smile and big attitude
I became her dude
Things seem to be at their best…
But there's a turning point and it all falls so fast
Would I change it if I could go back in the past?
I don't know, I thought I did what was right
I lost despite
A close friend getting a little too friendly wanting more than
friends
This is where the end begins
I consider her close but a line has to be drawn and understood
It is not you and I's names carved in the wood
It's me and her, her and me
So you and me pass what we are, can never be
Either we stay friends or we don't
But betray my lady I won't
I feel like I should tell her, no secrets
Or maybe I shouldn't but that puts me in a state of vex
And that's how I lost my lady
Who ever thought you'd get burnt by telling the truth
Her girls in her ear altering the story like a spoof
In their mind I had to have done something to provoke that girl's
feeling
They convinced my lady of that and therein lies the ending

The Struggle – Arctic

I don't love you any more, it's over…
Those words still surface on the beach of my mind
Like a dead fish fighting time
Slowly dying and eating away deep memories from the flesh
Memories of me at my best
Now when the moment gets deep, I turn heartless
Not totally thoughtless
…but close
The avoidance of pain and hurt is the excuse
The avoidance of suffering and abuse
From knowing the outcome and hanging my own noose
So I'm Davy Jones with my heart locked up tight
But not buried on an island, sunny and bright
It's in an ice cold fortress
Frozen and voiceless
Buried under, it's over…
Buried under, I don't love you…
Buried under, cold feelings
Buried under the arctic

The Struggle – The Best for You

Well I thought about you today
Wondering if everything was going your way
Wondering if you've found that guy to make you smile
Wondering...
Actually to be honest I hope not
I want the best for you but with me
That smile that lights up the day, I want to see
No one will have the connection that was ours
I know we'll never get past some scars
But I thought about us a few moments ago
I wish you the best, but not with some other guy yo

The Struggle – Never Hurt Again

I promised I'd never hurt again, I felt that pain
And I never wanted to feel the same
So I locked it all up, my feelings, my dreams, my heart…
If there's no wall to crumble how can things fall apart?
Right?
I'll never feel that hurt
So I'm a zombie, yeah that'll work
Living for just the basic needs in life
When a problem arises I don't need to fight
Because the outcome doesn't matter
I don't want to fall so I stay off the ladder
I promised myself, so I make no long term commitments
Losing out on a relationship, that pain is expensive
So if you need a care, sorry I ain't got it
I'm all out of it
My expenses are greater than my revenue and that equals no profit
If life is about risks, well I'm out that game
I'm taking no risk that will hurt me, that's my aim
Hey I don't hide it so I apologize if the feelings are one way
After he passed I made a promise to myself that day
I'll never feel that pain again

The Struggle – Elephant in the Room

She wants to be number one
The only one
It's obvious what it could be
But is it too be?
Is the one to be she?
Fighting for a spot I haven't made available
I can't say she isn't physically and mentally capable
I hate not being able to date her, but I love the space away though
I'll admit that one day so
Those feelings are still at the distance of a pole
What I'm not looking for keeps finding me
And I'm put in a position where I can lose love and a friend
After the curve there's a fall off and I'm close to the bend
The lows outweigh the highs
Well, in my mind's eye
I gave her my heart in hopes I'd return for it, and her
But I've kind of gotten used to not having it, not having her
What does that say about me and the absent feelings I hold?
The tardiness will get me suspended and be a story never lived, only told
She said if she can only have a piece of me
Then she has to say peace to me
In doing so she tears away a piece of me
Jay I don't wanna learn to live with regrets
But I have to seeing as though I lost those bets
In between the lines of our communication it's there
The elephant in the room

The Struggle – Keep it Real

Forgive me if I don't accept you with open arms
Don't be fooled by the charm
It's a defensive mechanism created by my self-conscience
A response to negative responses
No decision out of my hands will cause me to lose sleep
You can try but I'm in there deep
I'm not looking for a bad outcome, but that train is never late
Plan for the worst hope for the best; why wait?
Forgive me for not putting myself out there so fast
Never make the same mistakes twice, I've learned from the past
I'm trying to flip bad choices like reciprocal fractions
And hopefully leave a remainder for an exit against bad actions
I always keep it real, though I hold back
Yes, that's possible in my world
Accept that
Or don't, but that's all I got
Hopefully this isn't when keeping it real goes wrong
Because I see a few people walking away, long gone
I had a crowd like the man working for Verizon
Now they're disappearing into the horizon
See what happens when you keep it real
People say they want it but they don't
Stick around after you "keep it real" they won't
But keeping it real is all I've got

The Struggle – Just Because I'm Nice

Just because I'm nice doesn't mean I take advantage
This nice guy can manage
Just cause I'm nice and respond to her comment
Doesn't mean to her I'll commit
Just because I'm nice, I have nothing to prove
I do what I want, not to be rude
But I don't seek your approval
Just because I'm nice doesn't mean I'm easy to push over
I'm still on my toes and my stance is lower
I can take a punch
Just cause I'm nice doesn't mean I won't tell you no
Tell you you're not for me so go
Just because I'm nice don't think I don't see the real world
I'm just trying to adapt it to "my" world
Just because I'm nice
Don't think I'm covering up mean heights
God has blessed me with life
Change my personality I wouldn't for any price
I'm a gentleman, I'm nice

The Struggle – She Loves

She told me she loved me and I kind of felt bad
I kind of feel like I led her astray
I didn't intend for things to go this way
This early
I thought being upfront saying what I wasn't looking for would
work
But it may have worked against me
Because I enjoyed the time we spent together like no other
I felt comfortable, like a brother
Maybe a little too much so
Where I should've maybe fallen back, I moved forward
In my mind I stuck to the script and didn't give the wrong
impression
In my mind…
Maybe that didn't transfer into reality
Man… she loves me

The Struggle – Right or Wrong

Right or wrong I've given you me
The rest is up to you to see
I told you what was on my mind like you asked
I followed my heart so not to regret it once it's considered the past
But sometimes when I'm alone in my room I stare at the wall
Staring into myself I hear my conscience call
And I turn to answer but I'm driving with the windows down
In my rear view is Cleveland's downtown
My conscience is telling me something
Telling me to follow…
No, to find…
But the transmission is muffled and lost between my heart and mind
Rolling fast without the wheels, moving cars passing me bye
One keeps on passing blocking my view of the sky
I was driving away, how did she find me?
I guess I left tracks that made it easy
Right for taking the chance
Wrong for knowing I wasn't ready after just a glance
Right for sharing the experience of a highway cruise
Wrong for switching lanes when I drove and she was on snooze
Wrong for hitting the break and taking a sharp right
Exiting the vehicle and walking out of sight
Staring at the wall trying to make sense of my feelings, or lack there of
Right for taking the risk of the unknown
Wrong for the failure and the opportunity blown
I was just following my heart
…Am I wrong?

The Struggle – Solidarity

I never felt more alive
Then behind the wheel of my ride
Black on black Malibu, windows down
Tires peeling black top off the ground
I can't explain why I just love to float away, solo
American Eagle cargos and a polo
Just me and my own thoughts
Paying no attention, free cost
Mind, body, and soul gone
Seems I'm playing the game to play it
Gotta find what sparks me because everything is stale
Like life slipping away, skin pale
My thoughts are caged in a mental jail
Trying to divert myself from chasing love knowing the out come
But still surprised like, where'd her anger come from?
No matter if you tell 'em the truth upfront, the feelings lost mean
more
Losing the game they intended to win is heavy like the hammer of
Thor
A weight and a burden I also carry
It makes me weary
It makes it tough to ever love again
The allure of solidarity returns as my friend
And it keeps calling my name
I'm a prisoner of solidarity

The Struggle – Dark Place

Funny how life throws curves at you when you're not ready
You can be Albert in his prime and stand steady
Or fold and crumble, swing and miss
End up down in the dumps and the pits
What's the difference between a dark and bright place?
Either way you can't see what's ahead
And this is the ground I tread
I'm going backward on my forward progression
Going back to being buried after a resurrection
Pushing everyone and everything aside
Fighting to the death with my pride
You could say I'm in a dark place
But what's the difference when there's bright light in my face?
Is it just a feeling, happy verse sad?
Is it glad verses mad?
Motivated or depressed?
What does it mean to be suppressed?
In a dark place

The Struggle – Alone

Why do I feel so alone? For instance
Everyone is passing through my life or standing at a distance
They all come and go, take and leave
They hand me the tissue after they sneeze
They don't want me
I mean, they want me
But not for me
More like what I can do for them
They get mad when I tilt my brim
Turn my back and walk alone into the sunrise
It's like a costume party and everyone is in disguise
Did I create this ambience?
Or was it caused in the past by another presence?
Am I pushing them away in my defense?
Scared to open up as the plot thickens with suspense
Surprised when love gives me a glimpse
But what's so great about me, a flawed man?
A man sometimes scared to look passed his own hand
I struggle to keep balance and when I practice what I preach
I then hear, "I think I'm big Meech…"
And then I change like clear skies to snow
But you haven't known me long enough to say so
What if I never showed you the real me, how would you know?
This feeling of being alone is eating away at me but it's my
comfort zone
It's fully furnished with all my amenities, my home
To please everyone I think I'd need a clone
My actions may say otherwise, but I'm tired of feeling alone

The Struggle – My Everything

They say let no one become your everything
If you lose them, you lose everything
And I found out first hand
Giving her my heart with a golden band
She was my all
I was standing on a thin line hoping not to fall
She was the air I breathed
Whatever she wanted, I agreed
But she found something better
I was tossed like an old sweater
The new fix came along and I was done
Now it's dark with no sun
But there's a lesson in all things
And this was to trust not in human beings
Man will fail you where God won't
It's in men's nature to do so
But now my everything is in He who makes the wind blow
He'll never leave me because He's always around
He's there when I'm down
When I don't even realize
He sees me as a prize
I am a gift made to His glory
So not again will I put my everything in this Earth
All it does is rot away its worth
I put my everything in God and wait for His blessing
And everything will fall into place

The Struggle – Tearless Pain

Can you see the pain in my tearless cry?
Can you see the sincerity in my reason for wanting to fly?
I carry weight on my shoulders but I press on
I struggle to carry the cross for God's Son
In so much pain no tears will fall
But on the inside I ball
I call out to God asking my situation to change
He shows me I'm blessed and could be in a worse range
My own personal struggle, can you see it in my eyes?
Can you see what I try to protect and hide?
The mistakes and doubts of my path
The anger I feel and wrath
In my dreams asking Martin what to do
Asking Malcolm too
Should I go Huey P. or stand in Alex Haley's frame?
Stay in my Langston Hughes lane?
Or should I not even feel any pain, just keep it moving?
Wonder around not knowing what I'm doing
I shed tears for our ancestors looking down from on high
Seeing us not at our best and just getting bye
But I have to stand strong and show no fear
Continue to try and un blindfold the people so they can steer
Hustle for change, not the silver kind
The kind to uplift bodies, spirits, and minds
That's my charge, so I'll hold in my tearless pain
Because that alone won't cause change
Underneath this mask there is a painful face with dried tears
I haven't cried in years
When I do hopefully no pain will be involved

The Struggle – The Poem I Died In

It hurts me to my heart
To see the destruction of art
Our Queens are losing purity
I see it as obscurity
It's difficult to understand, what's wrong?
They starve for a day and go pick up that thong
And our brothers are nowhere to be found
We're running through this America bound
It's not even all by the racists
Its self inflicted hatred
Hating ourselves more than the people that made us slaves
Man Martin Luther King is turning over in his grave
Malcolm X going crazy thinking, "this is what I died for?"
Sugar coating the world won't help
But it's whatever makes life easier right? Whelp
It hurts me to my heart the world I'm viewing
I hope that American Pie cracks your teeth while chewing
For false advertising
We want our males to be G's and hustle hard
Our women to pop that for a VIP card
Give an inch, the world takes a yard
And our youth end up physically and mentally scarred
It hurts me to my heart to see this
And with a final gesture I clinch my fist
The pain of underachievement is killing me
…why isn't it killing you?

The Struggle – Anger

Man I'm so angry
You might not recognize me if you knew me since a baby
It's crazy
Everyone has two sides
I'm ready to do something unwise
I'm so frustrated and ready to blow
One wrong word and off the edge I'll go
It's not me by nature
But anger is the new flavor
This build up is deep like a meteor crater
I feel like a rapper trying to keep up the image
But it's not whole hearted, like a scrimmage
Just because I won't let anger get the best of me doesn't
mean I don't feel it
Its times people open their mouth and I want to seal it
But I can't let my people down
Before that, I'd rather drown
Yeah I'm a product of my environment
But I'm trying to live to see retirement
Anger is not a tool on my belt
It's collecting dust on the shelf
And the fight to keep it there ensues

The Struggle – Torched Soul

They all died…
They all just died…
My granddad died
I sat up all night with God and why'd
Why him? Why then? Just why!
My cheeks flooded from tears of my cry
Right there and then
I decided to build a dam and never flood again
Why Ma Middy? Why Papa?
My soul needs a doctor
And Papa was a dentist
Maybe he can help me with these feelings
If he was here…
I'm in a black out and can't steer
Hen for the pain
Make it a double for the anger
But what then helps with the hanger?
Is it really worth it? I don't care
Then cousin Nita
Tiza mi vida*
How'd I get the same feeling twice?
My heart's on ice
My soul is crispy, torched
It's confined to the porch
I'm trying to erase this pain with no eraser, where's Arnold?
Maybe he can set me free and I fly away like a cardinal
But I'm captured and caged
As I serve my sentence maybe peace comes from the page

*Chalk my life

The Struggle – Good Night Cruel World

Head in the pillow and my eyes open to a version of life
I'm literally living in the world of my dreams
When I open my eyes to this "real" world my boat loses steam
But when I close my eyes that kid that took two
Rises like a phoenix from ash or the morning evaporating dew
He lets us know to love freely whatever we do
Sometimes the cruelness of my heart gets heavy
Then there goes the levy
And in comes the flood
Sand bags sinking in the mud
Trying to escape so bad, my real life is in the dreams heights
Close my eyes and I see all of the lights
All the ones that matter in this life
Smiles of child birth
Fist pumps of under rated people showing their worth
Not letting their talents go for not
Digging a grave for negative thoughts to rot
Sleep walking eyes wide through this "real" life
Open my eyes to more death and losing of faith
But once you blink you can see God's grace
We selfishly leave God hollow
The people in our life from Him we borrow
And when they return to Him we feel sorrow
Good night cruel "real" world, see you tomorrow
Lay my head down, close my eyes
I'm going back to real life

The Struggle – The Mind of a Lonely Love

Laying here
Staring at the ceiling
Going over my options
As I take another shot
I've had enough to fill a semi automatic clip
And my mind is moving at a rapid tip
I'm falling for her and I can't get up the nerves
To tell her how I adore her curves
Her smile is a roof-less Maybach, amazing
Her mind is worth praising
Another shot
But what would make her choose me out of many men?
I bet her kiss would be like 0 to 60 type adrenaline
We're cool, we converse I wonder if she knows?
If she can sense how I feel
Sometimes I have to catch myself and fall back
As I throw another shot back
Waiting on her to text back
Maybe I should tell her that
But she's not like the rest and I want to handle this wisely
She's too good of a catch to have to throw right back because I
rushed
I'm feeling a little lust
She texts back but I can feel the liquor and I don't think this is the
right moment
To express my heart's intent
Every day is a missed opportunity and has a possibility of regret
Shots may call the bluff of my bet
But not today
Not in this mind of a lonely love

The Struggle – Grand Canyon

It's a disease to think of you
This much without the chance to be with you
I'm a grand canyon away from you
What shall I do?
Continue to dream?
Continue to try and script this theme?
Passing on all the others on this side of the canyon
Like settling for a bad shot, no chance of an and-one
I could jump the canyon or die trying
Will that fearless love catch me and start flying?
I don't know
The sun sets on your side of the canyon, amazing
The thought will again tomorrow walk my mind, grazing

The Struggle – Shouldn't Have Wrote

This is the poem I couldn't write
I stopped myself even when I thought I was so right
The fantasy is so real I couldn't stand her reading this
And then brushing right past it like a weak diss
Because this is my actual heart on these pages
We could be a love for the ages
The commonalities that we share
And the differences are fair
At your picture I could stare
I tried so hard to fight these feelings off
But sometimes they just bum rush you
And then she's all you can think about
Eventually arises that doubt
That says all that's against will hinder
The whole idea will be a painful after thought like the morning
after a binder
I should've never written this poem, it's just a reminder
And when she leads me on to find her
I'm too nervous to send that text
To make that call
Waiting on her to speak first may take too long
At least she'll know...
I should've never written this poem though

The Struggle – Hiding

I'm good at hiding it all
So what you think you know, is just that
What you 'think' you know
In all reality, you know nothing though
I'm a hard one to read and that is of my own doing
I've shaded the viewing
An event sent me on a different path with emotions
Rarely riding the same wave in my life ocean
I'm fighting
However, the waters are rough; I'm trying to keep it
together
Through crazy weather
I work at hiding and being good at it
Blocking any jab at it
Trying to control the uncontrollable brings forth varied
results
A lot of goes and halts
So my feelings for you, hidden
How mad I really was, hidden
We all adapt and react to situations differently
I went into hiding literally
Take it for what it's worth
Hopefully this is growth

The Struggle – Crack in the Wall

Staring at the wall
Staring at the crack in the wall
Staring at the crack in the wall in the living room
Staring at the crack in the off white wall in the living room
Staring at the wall and reflecting
Staring at the wall and reflecting back on that moment
Reflecting on that moment in time
That moment in time when I knew
When I knew what it was I was to do
That moment when it all came together
It was quiet, the eye of the storm in bad weather
It hit me like bricks
And burned like lots of Vicks
If we were to be a pair
Then it would be up to me to take that step there
But I'm stuck on the wall like a thrown dart
And I'm staring and ripping this wall apart
I was late; someone else beat me to her heart
So now it's just this wall and me

37

The Struggle – Catching Feelings

Every time I catch feelings I wash my hands
I shut off all the valves of the dams
The feelings move to another inbox like spam
Sorry

If I'm towards the ending stage of this funk I can't tell
I set forth on this path from the bottom, but I see no light top the well
Each brick and step is guided by a lady wishing more of me
Seeing more in me
Therefore wanting us more to be
But as I see
Just another step up towards the light
That probably isn't very polite
It's like two trains of thought in my mind on parallel tracks
They've separated and seem to never crash to link back
The 'was' and the 'who' of the man I wanna be
Soon
Logically thinking with emotional tendencies will lead me to doom
Until one catches me with that broom
The one that catches and holds debris
…how do I know she doesn't already know me?
I need to fall back before I catch feelings
But it seems

Every time I catch feelings I wash my hands
And those feelings get filtered out the dams
Sorry

The Struggle – Want From Me

She's yelling, "what do you want from me!?"
Tough to love consistently
With the threat of being hurt again
You befriend easy, but can't move past a friend
And when friends become more than
I become less than
Texts get shorter
Conversations get shorter
Time gets shorter
With my feelings I become a hoarder
What do I want out of this love thing?
Good question, where do I begin?
What's the rush on commitment
Love doesn't feel that sentiment
I take love, but can't give it
I can write it but tough to live it
Waiting on a fantasy that's stuck in a story book
But when the story was in my face, I didn't turn to look
I turned away
I turned away many and I'm afraid one will inflict karma
The consequences of my actions unfolding like a larva
Opening its wings and beautifully flying away
What am I afraid of? That day
(Continued)

I should be ready to take that leap
But I back off and go sheep
I try to indirectly show her a future with a future king
Where a beautiful queen wears a beautiful ring
I'd put all my fears to the side for this angel
Give me a sign and you can get the direct angle
I know she'd understand the struggle I bear
I wouldn't let her, but the pain she'd share
Looking to build something a lifetime couldn't separate
When they'd bring our names up, no debate
We are one and share each other's struggle
Loving hard, but hearts floating light as a bubble
But that's a dream in a bottle on the beach shore
I don't even know what I want out of love anymore
Maybe she'll show me

The Struggle – Almost Naked

I'm standing in front of her in nothing but a towel
Yeah, wow
No dripping water, no fresh shower scent
Just goose bumps caused by cool air coming from the vent
My clothes are laid out in front of me
She's folding them neatly
How kind right?
If only you knew how she stripped me down
Though through it all I never had a frown
Fully clothed and protected we began conversation
Every day thereafter was a certain anticipation
To see her words in bubble letters in my mind
Letting my imagination unwind
The idea of a woman like her and a guy like me
Asking God, could this one day be?
Can I really be slowly giving my heart away?
As the days turned to months, our connection grew closer
It became clear as a giant poster
Thoughts of her on my pillow and hopes of texts to wake up too
From a far off distance I wanted to be that dude
She began to strip away that outer layer I used to protect my heart
To explain I don't even know where to start
It was so gradual, that I'm now in this towel wrapped around my
waist
(Continued)

I wonder if she can see my nervous face?
I'm all exposed and at the mercy of her acquired taste
My seemingly impenetrable façade has been penetrated
That area is no longer gated
On the outside I'm a great guy
Hopefully that still stands after she gets past the shy
It's one thing to live the hype and another to live up to it
People like to see others as they want and not really are
Once naked she'll see my real heart and real scars
Even through my confidence nothing makes me more nervous
But then again if its Gods purpose…
Nothing more I can do but have patience
I'm almost naked

The Struggle – A Different Me

I'm seeing the change in me
The change others can't see
Well, they think they can
But as a man said, I've worked too hard not to change
Can't stay in that childish range
Got to grow up and explore
And in doing so you open up a new door
Or doors
Inside waging wars
Trying to figure what type man I'll be
Trying to find the real me
Looking for balance within
And looking away from her heels and grin
Temptation, so wrong its right
Especially at the height I like
A gentleman is for certain, but what's under the umbrella?
What makes me that type of fella?
There's a different me on the rise molded by failures, mistakes, and pain
Trying to wipe clean, where's the Gain?
As a person grows they can't stay the same
There are new situations to react too
New angles to view
Different shades of blue
If you're caught up in my changes accept my apology
I am only following my heart, logically
And, well, you know how hard that can be

The Struggle – Refitting the Mask

When we interact I wear a mask
Just in case my facial expressions move to fast
See I really care for you lady, more than I show
But that care I can't show
No not yet
So I use my mask to hide what's true
And what's true is I wanna be with you
…
I'm rocking this mask with a permanent smile to cover the frown
I'm a coward face down
Knees on the ground
I should be telling you how I feel
So we can see what's the deal
I shouldn't be worried about rejection and circumstance
I should be asking for your hand in this dance
…
Refitting the mask so it fits snug
I'm not the man you thought I was
The mask lets me mask what's true
And what's true is I'll rob you
I'll get your guard down and take your heart
I'll take it to my shop and rip it all apart
But then I'll put it on the mend starting the recovery process
Making it stronger in order to handle the stress
See the mask was to represent those who hurt you in the past
And I remove to show you the pain won't last
The mask was for the surgery of repair
Now you can see my face, not only my hair
I'm not trying to be Prince Charming rushing in to save the day
Or that dream man that does things the exact right way
Rather I just wanna be your man, in reality
Flawed but loving you adequately
Refitted

The Struggle – Always Smiling

The embodiment of joy she was
Slang word, she was my "cuz"
But more so like an aunt
Even close to god mother
She was like no other
Every time I saw her she smiled at me
She called me cutie repeatedly
Always told me she was proud
She followed me like a cloud
When I was down, I always knew she was praying
Praying for me to succeed
A kind Angel, the best breed
She'll always be a part of my soul
In my heart she always has a role
Days turn to months, a short time into a while
I will always remember that smile

Love you cousin Nita

The Struggle – Storm from the Outside

His life is slipping away; still he wants me to eat
She has to tend to him I should be last on her check sheet
I see now
Someone else's storm can positively change
I couldn't accept because I had to grow my frame
Pain was internalized instead of seeing the big picture
It took my own storm and hard rain
It took a fall so I could stop using it like a cane
Viewing their storm from the outside opened my eyes
It suddenly became clean like clearing of the skies
Being positive in your storm can help motivate another through
theirs
My grandparents didn't have to care
They didn't have to share
While they were going through their storm

The Struggle – Self-Esteem

You probably wouldn't think I struggle with self-esteem
But why blame others, its self-esteem
I sit back and question myself
The stress adds up to bad health
I don't think I can do it
But God will see me through it
How could a skinny dude like me get her and keep her
She'll settle for me, sure
My stature is too small
So people think I can't ball
One drop of doubt could ruin a cop of confidence
But I got it back, God took over my sponsorship
And I'm running with it
I'm staying on the path, why skip it?
With this Champ in my corner I can do anything
I don't have to fear what tomorrow will bring
With that in my mind I'm not afraid to fail
In that way I can come out my protective shell
Self-esteem no longer gets me down
Now I can strive to be the best pound for pound

The Struggle – Under the Pale Moon Light

I'm stuck in this 2-step dance; salsa turned waltz
The craziness in my mind I can't control with my thoughts
I'm not the leader in this dance
And if you've never danced this dance
You wouldn't understand this trance
Feeling like a fallen angel
There is no right angle
I'm going in circles… eyes blurry… head spinning
Ever so often I see my dance partner grinning
These steps I can't control
D'Evils are on a roll
I can't blame the evils, because as a man I'm accountable
I can't blame this figure in a purple get up
I hold power like a volcano, I just got to erupt
There's no easy out, just through
There's always a way to release from glue
However, this is my struggle and you may not understand
If you could take my pains and make them yours
    You still couldn't grasp them with a firm hand
Everything slows down when I take control of the dance
"Have you ever danced under the pale moon light Marc?"
I reply, "Yes, and it's just enough light to brighten the dark"

The Struggle – Soul Searching

"A lot of people black, white, Mexican, young, old, fat, or skinny have a problem being true to themselves. They have a problem looking in the mirror and looking directly into their own souls."
2Pac

The mirror is looking at me, right in my eyes
Questioning my size
The size of my heart and the level of my fear
So afraid of being seen I steer away from the clear
I shift in and out the shadows, staying near the tree line
But I have a light to shine
I have to overcome that fear I see in my eyes
Look to the raining skies
And let God wash away that doubt
It's on me to sacrifice self for others
Time to remove the covers
My flaws and short comings will uplift someone I don't know
That's part of life yo
If I don't inspire someone who will?
We walk through life just walking
I want to walk with a purpose
I'm looking in the mirror taking control
Following my soul
And making plans for a bigger role

The Struggle – From the Pulpit

As the saying goes, practice what you preach
Live the ways that you teach
I've failed
And I can try to justify these failures
I should ask you to share yours
But we all struggle
Sometimes it's all about who can juggle
Standards are high for a reason
To let them down is treason
It's easy to give in, just this once
An adrenaline junky I'm ready for rush
Once leads to twice and an unpaved road
Leading to no gold
Just disappointments and let downs
Smiles in the moment, lead to frowns
Knowing the right way and going left
Leaves outsiders seeing you as inept
Have some perspective, it's an everyday struggle
Sometimes that's just an excuse for not being able to juggle
I'm a man, I'm flawed. But I want to move boulders
God gives His hardest tests to His strongest soldiers
I'm still going to try to lead the way
That's all I can do at the end of the day
Be accountable

The Struggle – Changing Around Me

I'm struggling with the man I'm becoming
Almost like from it I'm running
Trying to hang onto the world when it won't hold me
My season is changing like the leaves of a tree
Rake 'em up and move on
God didn't send his son
For me to continue down this path
It's easy math
So I thought
All I'm doing is lying to Him
So God, I stopped praying to Him
Glad he didn't give up on me
Down and out He's Ray Allen for a corner three
Jesus
The world will wither and die
Eat its heroes alive
It's now or never
Give it up forever and ever
And let God command my struggle
Rising from the rubble
A different me
Not confined by this ever changing world
This give a little, take a lot world
Stand firm while all is changing around me

The Struggle – Pouring Out

Find myself in a tall glass
Steady sips as time pass
As each sip goes down and the glass drains
Goes with it are my pains
My insecurities and fears
My secrets and missing gears
The bottom is here and I'm being poured out
But just when it seems a drought
I'm poured out onto the page
There I become a sort of sage
Letting all my humans fears fall by the way side
Becoming wise and overcoming my pride
Spilling out I let it all go
I let all my emotions show
I'm at my most vulnerable
I'm pouring out my soul
It's hard but I'm trying to maintain control
No holding back because I'm behind closed doors
Blood from my knees all over the floors
Remember I got poured out, knees first
God I thirst
What's being poured ain't drink
Coming up and out are those mentioned a few lines ago
Hopefully throwing up my ego, also
You may not see it when you look in my eyes
But I'm pouring out my insides

The Struggle – No Tomorrow

If I were to die tomorrow I want my folks to know they were everything
From my born day in spring
Till I rested my eyes
I wanted to be just like them, wise
Kept a clear head and followed my heart
Using some emotion but not letting it lead the cart
Followed God and kept family above all
I love y'all
If I go tomorrow and that's it and in God's presence I sit
Don't worry even a little bit J you'll always have my spirit
If I were to leave this Earth tomorrow
Those that cared feel no sorrow
My time here was borrowed
And to you I wish I could've expressed true feelings
I hid behind friendship and pride in our dealings
To let my grandfather's pain go I wasn't willing
Bad timing
For I wanted to give you the world after a short time meeting
But with my baggage and pride, couldn't muster up that greeting
Not sure if you knew so I'll leave it at that
Tomorrow isn't promised
So if you had a negative thought about me
Forgive me
As much as telling those you love, that you love them
It's important to end grudges and petty disagreements
Life is too short
This is my PSA before there's no tomorrow
And I have to give back to God that which I borrowed

The Struggle – Confined to Poetry

I thought she was the one to cure me
The one to pure me
Purify me
I had nightmares of life, love, and loss
These thoughts and emotions I couldn't toss
Then this chick came into my life
I had to look twice
How did I get so fortunate?
I thought she would take me to glory
I'd even take Robert Horry
She's been studied from the block to the lecture hall and more over
I was new; I brought her joy even though on the list I was lower
But quickly she rose to the top, of the game
Fizzing over her like a can of pop, what a shame
The can shook and exploded
My heart got agitated and folded
She was supposed to set me free
The present is a gift and I just wanna be
I gave up my heart to her with total faith
With a straight unapologetic face
Ten, Jack, Queen, King, and I just pulled the Ace
Well, so I thought
Blinded by the compliments I get when in her presence
Not knowing I was viewed like peasants
She used me for my soul on paper
And tossed me sooner than later
I thought I was using poetry, but poetry used me
She trapped me and I set her free
(Continued)

Now I'm stuck spilling my feelings in rhyme
And not in real life, in real time
But I can't leave her, she's so fine
Too bad no one cares
Quickly changes the time and stress grey go the hairs
She was good with hamburger helper
I tried to upgrade her to fillet mignon and develop her
I tried to give her my all, but that'll never be enough
Trapped in poetry now
I've given my vow
But she runs around with others
They feel inspired and become lovers
Now I have to share because I'm not letting go
I'll cut them down first like a kid in a barber's chair with a fro
It's tough though
I'm trapped though
Trapped by my own writing
It was suppose to be enlightening
But some of it I can't even read
It brings on hard memory seeds
Geez
How did poetry entrap me?
She used me
…and I love every minute of it

The Struggle – Tears of My Mother

Tears running as I hear her speak
They're not mine, but going down my cheek
Tears of my mother hold so much emotion
The joy or pain affects me the instant her voice cracks
How do I handle that?
She cares so much for her kids
If her pain could go in a jar I'd have dibs
To release her from her struggle and her stress
To give her a sense of rest
I'm first born
That's my torch to carry
Even when my shoulders are weak
It's my promise to keep
I can never repay mom for whom and what she is
For what she means
Hopefully I can shade her with some money trees
I just can't stand to see those tears of stress
I drop to my knees feeling less than less
Helpless
Powerless
God help her and remove my fears
Of seeing my mother's tears

The Struggle – A Good Man

A good man is gone, but not forgotten
On revenge I was kind of plottin'
But it's all God's plan
Though that's tough to comprehend for a young man
Even harder when he goes while you're close
In proximity, how's that for a dose
Of reality
Been about ten years; a good man is gone
He's probably next to God on His throne
No one made me laugh like this man
He rivaled Bill Cosby as a handyman
I mean, duck tape to stop kitchen sink leaks
Permanent solutions, not just tweaks
Strong and sturdy, but graceful as a dancer
Robbed of life by cancer
A good man is gone
The biggest heart and most funniest of them all
He saved my fish by almost taking a fall
He sank a 30 foot putt with no practice; walked off tall
Entertainer, he embodied it
The jokes and the smiles I see like yesterday
Though my dad and uncles describe a different way
An authoritative figure, quick to discipline
But he was thinking, "oh those boys again"
I wish he could've held my little love
But maybe he was there when God sent her from above
(Continued)

A good man is gone
Yet always in my heart
His soul will never part
Some memories fade with age
But somehow it sticks with me, the final stage
To see Superman's father weak and vulnerable
It's horrible
It brings tears to my eyes even now
I try to erase these times with the positives
But man, something has to give
When the struggle gets going he comes to mind
Still some peace is hard to find
I try to laugh during the tears
And stand tall in my fears
Fears of feeling that lose again
And taking a Tyson fist to the chin
I'll leave it to God's discretion
Why a good man is gone

The Struggle – Eclipse

August 7, 2012 the sun shines brightest
The joy is at its highest
The first cry to let us know she lives
What joy that gives
The first time she blinks and smiles
That feeling is wild
The joy on all their faces is real, no debate
This feeling was worth the nine month wait
The first laughter and first crawl
The first time standing with support from the wall
The first steps lead to running and not walking
And loud noises that aren't talking
Then the poop that starts to smell
The spoiled cries and tantrum spells
The eclipse rises with the fears
Insecurities of capabilities holding back tears
Lots of expectations to live up too
It is to me, but its not all new
But dark doubts slow creep
And I often lose sleep
What if she fell?
That's a few minutes of hell
How about when she cries in pain?
How can I not go insane?
What about when she starts to pout?
Will I have the strength to wait it out?
All of a sudden the light shines again
These thoughts do blend
But with my great family
That always stands by me
There's always light in the dark
Time will tell if I've left my mark

The Struggle – Purpose Greater than My Own

Watching my little princess take these steps
God bless
He has bestowed upon me more than a gift
It's a major life shift
A responsibility unlike any other
I'm all over her like a cover
Protection, guidance, comfort, and love
God has passed me one of his doves
Precious
While being in the unknown
I'm not falling into a hole
My drive has increased
I want to be a beast
Leave a legacy she can be proud of
But not missing the greater purpose above
All other things monetary in this world
Everything goes back to my little girl
I have a greater purpose than my own

Watching my little princess sleep
Wondering if she counted sheep
My life shifted after I graduated
And again after J's mom was impregnated
A year into fatherhood and I'm still scrambling
Feeling like every choice is like gambling
All I know is I love my baby girl
No one can pave this path for you
But Jorden this for you
This book is for you
This struggle is for you
(Continue)

Looking at you thinking, "isn't she lovely"
Those cheeks are so chubby
All I want to do is give you the globe
At least the correct signs on the road
Leading to a full and exceptional life
Looking at you rest, I have to face my fears
Can't hide these real tears
Don't want no momma drama
Just want to be the best like the Mamba
I have a greater purpose than my own

61

The Struggle – Dear Lord (Confession)

Dear Lord this is… Well it's me
I am coming bowed down to thee
I am coming to you stripped and broken
Worth less than a token
Dear Lord hear my prayers
See me true, beneath all the layers
I shouldn't be granted any of Your grace and mercy
I shouldn't be granted water when I'm thirsty
But I come to You on my knees, a humble servant
Looking for the forgiveness I know I don't deserve it
Going through life with a care free faith
Oh, I've got time to change my face
But what about when the ships down and I'm lost in space?
I am closer to God as a saved man, yet still lost
Since He paid the ultimate, couldn't I pay a small cost?
Dear Lord, hear my confession and touch my heart
Give me the strength and the faith to do my part
If I make one step towards You
Towards me You'll take two
Dear Lord, forgive me of my sins and wipe me clean
Of my life I want You to be the theme
Sincerely me, Your child

The Struggle:

Through (My) Eyes of the World

"Change does not roll in on the wheels of inevitability, but comes through continuous struggle." –
Dr. Martin Luther King, Jr.

The Struggler

I am the Struggler
You are the Struggler
We are the Strugglers

The kids wanting to attend college to break a negative stereotype
But the people around them who've done nothing say it's all hype
It's a dream wrapped in a metal pipe

The white kid raised around blacks
But not being accepted enough to receive dap
All their frustrations placed upon this kids' cap

I am the Struggler
You are the Struggler
We are the Strugglers

The guy who can't get passed his own demons to let her in
She wants nothing but to love him but he sees the ice as thin
He sees the act of giving away his heart as a loss and not a win

The girl who wants to take a chance on him but something says no
Neither will come out and say it but both are hungry for love like a
hippo
He lays down crumbs for her to follow to his heart but a hard wind
blows
(Continued)

64

I am the Struggler
You are the Struggler
We are the Strugglers

The struggle of being true to your word by living actions
Weeding out the unhealthy passions
And the accepting of breaking yourself down like fractions

The struggle of going out on a limb and failing
That business opportunity closing sail and never sailing
That girl dropping your heart and bailing

We are the Strugglers

Can You Hear

MLK bumpin' out my speakers, can you hear the dream?
All black Malibu, I call it dark King, black empowerment is the theme

It was written long ago for this king to have existed
Stated through the sands of times in hieroglyphics
I'm starving I got a whale stomach, never full
I'm the tide; greatness is the direction of its pull
Broken alignment of kings from golden thrones in jungle and desert
Seeing us grovel in doubt and without self respect
Steering our queens into a devastating train wreck
I'm only one man, but I too have a dream
As MLK's voice blasts out the speakers sending chills like I was there that day
I'm following the dream in my own way
A way I hope to share with those with dying dreams
Sprinkle in some LASERS beams
See them grow like a beautiful spring day after the strife
Today is the next day in the days of the rest of your life
The change starts with you

Bob Marley bumpin' out my speakers, can you hear the dream?
All black Malibu, I call it peace, black unity is the theme
(Continued)

Infuse some peace into your soul
Seek with open eyes your role
Be a blessing to someone else, someone else will be a blessing to you
It doesn't matter the who
Keep your mind and heart open to God
And God will fill it with peace, love, and a healthy pride
You have a voice that will affect someone
And you never know who will be that one
I only want to uplift and inspire
Encourage to have faith strong as a thin wire
Holding up a ton of bricks
Burning strong like a candle wick
I want to aspire to a past but not live in it
Learn from those who came before
Readjust our wings so we can sore
Your self-esteem wouldn't be low if you knew your God's power
If you knew your worth
You descended from the first people on this Earth
You got soul, you're super bad

James Brown bumpin' out my speakers, can you hear the scream?
All black Malibu, I call it super bad, black soul is the theme

Queen of Sorrow

She's so dramatic
Everything is crafted
She puts on a show
To show you she's feeling low
She gets into relationships
Just for the hardships
She likes being a woman scorned
You've been warned
She's the queen of sorrow

Woe is me is she
You know how it be
This man and that man ain't squat
You don't want to be in that spot
Broken hearted so many times
Her heart now hides behind blinds
Instead of moving forward, she's in park
She likes the attention that shines on her in the dark
You've been warned
She's the queen of sorrow

She lets men in, but only in the foyer
They see her heart only through a digital display
But what happens when one gets through?
That one fly dude
She can't deny love forever
Love is way too clever
But she has found ways to mess up before
For her it's not that hard a chore
But how long can she be the queen of sorrow?

Comfortable (In Hell)

She's dancing in a burning room
Burning the candle at both ends with a bubbly spoon
She only cares about the heat of the moment
She's not looking for atonement
She's dancing these steps without a care
She pushes people away until she needs them
Until they fan the flame and it's no longer dim
She makes the most of the flame
With no shame
When everyone else is comfortable, she's not
She's only comfortable when her veins are hot
When she's in an alley or busted house, eyes rolled back
Her mind drifts and fades to black
People who've loved her can't understand
Her new lifestyle they're not a fan
She's going through hell and they can't break the spell
But some people are more comfortable in hell

69

Under the Law

She gets more stopped cars than a stop sign
Never in her life has she been wined and dined
The most romantic thing a guy has done is wear protection
Sad isn't it
Undercovers with badges give chase
They split up as her four inch heels go with haste
One catches her, cuffs in hand pushing her against the fence
The moment is intense
She can't go to jail
Her employer won't give bail
She pleads the only way she can, offering her body catching his
lust
How can any man deny her touch?
Her eyes use to be beautiful and bright
Now they look like they've given in to the night
He looks both ways before indulging
Hearts pulsing
The deal is he gets what he wants and her he'll protect
Sounds like more pimp-ish dialect
He emerges and says, "Partner, she gave me the slip."
Partner says, "Aight pimp"
Funny…
Now she's back to stop-signing
In her dark struggling moments crying
Under the law

What She Needs

She likes what I'm offering
But I'm not offering what she needs
Short life span is the span for these seeds
There's no wisdom and growth in our interaction
Just a money transaction
Just enough to keep her a float
But not enough to maintain the boat
She can get some new clothes, fly and all
But without education only thing she'll grow is tall
She likes the feeling but the feeling isn't what she needs
She needs inception to give her a new idea to breed
Pleasing her mind instead of these money tossing guys
Sprinkle in some salt, she's just large fries
We all know what the potential can be
But she has to want to see what we see
We all want her to do more with life then put her hands on
her knees
But then who are we to tell her what she needs

What She Needs (In Her Words), By Devonie Newton

What you're offering is cool
      But see it's not what I need
Education and pencil skirts
      See that's not really my speed
I'm a descendent from the old school
      The last of a dying breed
Not a female dog of any kind
      But I know how to get what I need
A little switch in my behind and those dollars are mine
I can slick talk and charm without wasting time
A future is what I should plan for, but I'm living for the
now
Your, "I have a dream" speech is nice, but it's only telling
me how
Not giving me what I need
Just giving me hopes and dreams
For now it's hustle by any means
The only one that I got is me
To give me what I need

Lost Diamond

Wipe her clean and see the diamond potential
But showing her the way isn't so simple
She's a jewel, but doesn't know it yet
And she's naïve to this game of chess
She thinks their warnings are to impede her progress
But they just want her to have success
They wanna give her the tools and strength to build whatever
They want her to be smart and clever
But she brushes it off her shoulder not looking at who is at her side
She just wants a seat in the ride

She's becoming a black girl lost
Selling herself for a cost
She's any color, not just black
She gives up what's priceless
Just to have "girls" and a dude to say she's the nicest
She's lost and instead of playing the cards in her hand
She wants to fold and lay up under a man
Friends start to pressure her about waiting till marriage
But she knows about what could happen, baby in a carriage
She's used to a fall back person, but she's alone
And she has too much pride to pick up the phone and call home
Stressed and confused
Hopefully she's still strong enough not to get used
She feels like she can't say no
To her fast friends she can't be slow
It's more than videos and gossip
More to the cup than a hot sip
It's easier to go along than go alone
But her goal should be to be queen of her throne
Young princess let your mind shine like lip gloss
Don't be a diamond lost

Gettin' Over on Her

She keeps loving the dudes that keep screwing her over
She's a Beyonce type, but keeps dating lower
They see Jay, but they forget the growing up part
They forget Jay said soon she'll understand to do better than
him
Better than them
She still gives her heart freely
But she knows something is wrong secretly
That intuition is a powerful tool if paid attention too
Not always true
But no one knows you better than you
And that inner you knows what's best
But she falls for the troubled past looking to change but can't
give up the past
No matter how hard she tries it won't last
He's been dealing with tricks his whole life, he doesn't know a
Queen
And it's not up to her to teach him such a thing
Long as she keeps giving these guys rope they'll keep hanging
her
Then mean mugs outweigh smiles and the love seems a blur
As if it never were
Don't bring the rope
Make them earn your hope
Make them jump through hoops
Who enters your heart should be a limited and elite group
They'll call you stuck up, but not "the one that got screwed
over"

Different

She's so contrary to popular belief
You wouldn't want to give up on her lease
Her name even tastes different when spoken off the tongue
She gives my favorite food a run
And there's no intention for a pun
This is "real talk" even though cliché
My ears are on the lookout for anything she may say
I say contrary because she's beautiful but her mind shines
She stands tall as pines
And she's all m…
Well maybe not
But I would like her to be the main character in my plot
My story
She can be my Robert Horry
People fear words like different, strong willed, independent
But of royalty we're all descendent
She's different, not compared to the latest video
When seen out, people don't go "here we go"
Here we go with the same 'ol mini dress
Same 'ol shirt revealing a well lotion chest
She's a beautiful lady with curves nonetheless
But she doesn't have to show her butt or breasts
She's so different
Complex even, meaning it takes time to understand her
She's not simple, making guys uneasy or unsure
But that's what I like about this lady
…even if she's not meant for me
Just to know she's out there is great
And just because she's different doesn't make her fake
She's just different

Open Book

Can't judge a book by its cover
So to get a better look I open her cover
From the introduction I read beauty and intelligence
A sense of womanhood, a strong presence
The cover is a sight to see in itself
But open the book to obtain much more wealth
She is a page turner
And I'm a fast learner
Page after page I read about love
And that she needs a little shove
Her heart shines as I read more
This book she authored is far from a bore
This is how you fall in love with a book
Reading into and not going by the look
The cover just brings you in
So an inside beauty that matches outside beauty is a real win
I see a woman's growth
The rising and falling slope
Each year in life is a new chapter to write and read
Looking for a good book; fellas take heed
Her life reads like an open book
Be careful, her pages will have you hanging from a hook
To enjoy completely you have to read
You need to show interest and plant that seed
Or it'll get cut short like a weed
Cover to cover her open book breathes life
Nice

Hey Sista

Walked up on this lady at the lounge
The scene was profound
Tears in her eyes, shot glass empty
No words came, but then simply
Everything ok baby girl?
She said not in her world
Took a seat and gave an ear
Her eyes were full of fear
Doubt of her path for life
Losing faith in everything, even Christ
Couple babies, couple baby's dads
She's in a barrel full of crabs
The people around her won't let her rise
And no one hears her cries
Two jobs and still not enough
Life is rough
She's lost the worth her soul holds
She's put it away like a poster with folds
Drowning her pain in a small glass
Too small to hold the problems of her past
And too full of the past to hold the future
But once she realizes she's a beautiful and intelligent creature
She won't need a glass to fill
Because the heart will hold without spill
But that's a road she couldn't see at the moment
...all I could say was

Hey sista, keep ya head up
After the rain the sun comes up
Keep smiling, move, and don't sit and wait
Ten steps from God, take two and He'll take eight
Now you're two steps past your problems

Lost One (Again)

Might win some but she just lost one
And with that her soul goes from full to almost none
While she hides it, she leaves her heart on her sleeve
That's a fact her man doesn't have to believe
So not maintaining happiness with someone hurts her to her
insides, her soul
But she promised to herself not to let it take a toll
Trying to be an everything woman while not letting her own flaws
shine
But she can't be everything to everyone at the same time
She's not perfect by any stretch but she tries to give of her freely
But she can't always do it completely
So now she has to sweep those feelings under a rug with a back log
of other feelings...
That's where feelings and lost ones lie
The bulge in that rug is getting pretty high
Man...
She is just a woman and doesn't pretend to be anything more
She's always going to fall to expectations of anything more
And the moment she does, she's kicked out the door
Well... Ok
Burger King, she says have it your way
Stupid emotions and expectations get one in trouble
And they got her again, bartender make that a double
Somebody is going to file malpractice on her soon
She just lost another one, she asks for the broom

Sick of Dying

I'm sick of dying
Sick of tearless crying
Every time I hear her name
I feel more pain
And I die all over again

That scent is her scent
That doorway she came and went
Every time my heart is stopped
Those arteries can't be unblocked
And I die all over again

The pain of love thoughts
The agony of love lost
Every time I think, it hurts
If you've loved, you know how it works
No one after can compare
You compare them down to their hair
It's all out of fear
Fear that you don't know where to steer
Fear of losing another love
You know the damage it does
And you don't want to die again

Coming Back for More

She hates him
Absolutely hates him
That smirk he gives after a smart comment
The anger is so prominent
The jerk moves he possesses
But yet she undresses
It's those same traits that make her heart flutter
She bounces back like rubber
And she keeps coming back for more

She pays him no attention except when she needs
And into her propaganda he feeds
He's at attention when she calls
Her voice travels through walls
He tells his boys he's tired and feed up
They say well, man up
But every time he walks out the door
She whispers to him in his thoughts and he comes back for more

It dilutes its people
And keeps them unequal
You're standing on a step stool and still can't reach the top shelf
To achieve what it supposedly holds you'll waste your health
It's a marriage that flickers in the light and lights up bright at night
It's embedded deep in our minds core
The American Dream tricks us every time, but we keep coming
back for more

On My Mind

It's so much on my mind I can't think straight
Life's thoughts piling up at my gate
With nowhere else to roam
Looking like the lawn of a gutted home

She's on my mind a lot lately
And my mind drifts and travels to future thoughts
That are probably premature at best
But they are the best
Of thoughts
I don't want to call her perfect
Because there's more of her to explore
More depth to delve and dive into
With no life jacket drowning in her being
Her soul
Deep right
Always knew I'd one day come round to these feelings
And that time has come
Life is a beach with ample sand
And out of all the grains she stands out
Now how do I go about expressing to her?
What she probably already can tell
The King in me has to come through
(Continued)

It's so much on my mind I can't think straight
Life's thoughts piling up at my gate
With nowhere else to roam
Looking like the lawn of a gutted home

All of this is spilling off the top of my dome
Through the skin and hair
Dripping down my forehead and down my face
Steady drops on the page
Filling it with thoughts I can't say
All my fears, ambitions, prayers, and joys
Some thoughts take longer to drop
My heart goes out to Trayvon's family
He deserves justice, but he's just one angle
Once we stop killing ourselves
Our lives will mean more
The system is killing us slowly
But we're speeding up the process
Instead of attacking the system by twos
We take one out to be the only one
But that makes its easier to be pushed back
It's not easy when we're all qualified
They can't deny us then; they can't deny us now
So how do I get my message out?
The King in me has to come through

It's so much on my mind

Land of the Frozen Sun, By Raheem Stanfield

"Chosen one from the land of the frozen sun" —Common *Be*
(Intro)

I walk outside
And see the breath of my people
Exhaling the worries and strife of their reality
'Cause I'm from the land of the frozen sun
The fire's dim in our eyes
So we turn to the one's that can't cry
To ignite a flame and feel warmth from somewhere
'Cause this is the land of the frozen sun
There are no revolutionary thinkers
So our shoulders are slumped from the beating of oppression
And all we can do is participate in the race to raise our arms
In preparation for this cold war
'Cause we are in the land of the frozen sun
Hungry for knowledge
We have no food for thought
So we settle for whatever we can get our hands on
Drinking as fast as we can the public education milkshakes
provided for us.
While the suburban kids get mental nourishment from a hot meal,
We're left with brain freeze
'Cause we're inhibited by the land of the frozen sun
We can't get jobs with decent pay
So how can we fare well,
When welfare is just a light jacket with holes in it?
And we're still in the land of the frozen sun
(Continued)

Our snow is looked at as dirty
So no plows are coming through
Leaving cars snowed in,
Bikes are broken,
And no walking 'cause our spirit has collapse due to high wind
So we're stuck in the land of the frozen sun
Our days are dim
Our nights are dark
And the glimmer of hope
Has been frozen over by the temperature of the shoulder in which
we show each other
'Cause this is the land of the frozen sun
But on we will walk
Resilience is us
Living through adversity with the blood of a slave
Marching on with the heart of a King
So there will be one,
Whose fire shall burn bright enough to lead
But who will be this chosen one from the land of the frozen sun?

Struggles, By Tommie Lee Stanfield, III

Some people complain that life isn't fair
People who use food stamps don't care
They're putting food on the table
And other families aren't able
To do the same
Some rich people just think it's a game
Seeing who can make the most money and competing for fame
But I think we should be paid the same
Man the struggle is real
People not having enough money to get a meal
They can't find a good deal
So their only option is to starve or steal
That's not what they want for their life
It's terrible out there
It makes you want to burst into tears
And it's been happening for years
People still ignore it like it's not an issue
It's so bad out there. People crying; somebody go get them a tissue
Or some food, some money, and house
If we're making wishes, than I would wish them a good spouse
But of all these wishes, many people would try to douse me
Because my dreams are like fire, once it's out of control
They can't stop me
I want us all to be rich
I'm going till it happens

Langston Hughes Wrote

This ain't the way Langston Hughes wrote us
There's a way out the struggle, just trust
    Hold fast to dreams, for if dreams die
    Life is a broken-winged bird that cannot fly
The dream of King is still evolving
We're outside math class still problem solving
But some of us won't take advantage of education
Not all doors open, but a lot do after graduation
We can't dry up like a raisin in the sun
We have to dream on cause the rain will come
We'll be rejuvenated and challenged again
The rain is our enemy, the rain is our friend

I'm looking at the news around dusk
This ain't the way Langston Hughes wrote us
Killing one another instead of building
A powerful culture with no limits like an open ceiling
Remember the rain is going to come, embrace it
Lift your hands, open wide and taste it
    Let the rain kiss you and beat upon you with silver drops
    Let it sing you a lullaby like the voice of your pops
Beautiful black people loving one another down to the crust
This is the way Langston Hughes wrote us
(Continued)

Langston Hughes saw the atrocities happening to black men
Trayvon is another straw in the casualties of those men
    I swear to the Lord, I still can't see
    Why democracy means, everyone but me
    Negroes – Sweet and docile, meek, humble and kind
    Beware the day they change their mind
But when the camel's back breaks it cannot be an outpour of only violence
That only creates more silence
I can't see people caring and valuing our lives when we don't
We love trends; Jenna 6, Trayvon, black power, go vote
Not soon after, we're back to the regularly scheduled program
Where's the national uproar of blacks killing blacks?
We want to fight the man
While sticking to his plan
Langston Hughes didn't write us ignorant and divided
He didn't write us non-educated and one sided
Langston Hughes wrote us beautiful and royal
He wrote us powerful and loyal
He planted seeds of growth in our soil
Ever flowing like a river changing and growing like the tide
Strong in unity and compassion, healthy pride
It's up to us to continue the way Langston Hughes wrote us

My Back is Strong

"I am the American heartbreak-
Rock on which Freedom
Stumps its toe-
The great mistake
That Jamestown
Made long ago."

-Langston Hughes

I am the American heartbreak
The back freedom stands on
It pees on my head and calls it rain
Its suppose to represent hard times and growth
To get a glimpse I have to look at its reflection in the puddle
My back is strong
But to really see freedom I have to turnover
In doing so I shake up the status quo
Then I'm called a thief, a criminal, a ni--er
When I'm only trying to be as free as the next
I am the rape of my Motherland to a murderous regime
I am the next generation, its offspring
I am American heartbreak
But songs of my broken heart are what America rocks too
"And for that paper look how low we'll stoop/
Even if you in a Benz, you still a ni--a in a coupe"*
But it's cool, because in that reflection I see the dream from a
different angle
Don't worry about us, our backs are strong

*quote by Kanye West

Legacy

What legacy do we leave?
What legacy will we leave?
What type of seed do we breed?
We should be leaving ones worthy of Queens and Kings!
Not just currency and rings
Stories of glory, culture, and myths
But we leave single parents and daughters shaking their hips
We leave cars with sounds that are all base
We leave kids to be raised at moms' place
We should be leaving dreams of space
Dreams of uplifting an entire culture
But we think as if a vulture
Won't lend a hand because we're waiting to take what the next person has
Sacrifice for another, we'll pass
When will we open our eyes to see how behind we are?
But glancing at that big booty, we rather follow that to the bar
We'll go broke trying to get that instead of investing in our kid's future
Being in America it'll be hard for us to gain wealth but there is a wealth of knowledge to be passed down
Don't let the legacy go crashing to the ground

Conversation

We just want the conversation
Not the alienation
The older generation thinks we're lost
The significance of our short history should be tossed
They think we're all Jordan's, whips, and chains
We're knuckle headed scarecrows without a brain
It's more too it; there's real pain
If they'd help finish the brick road we can ease on down
Ease on down, the road
What do you expect when you introduce money to a poor people
with no upward leadership?
Instead of investing, those kids gone ride around and spend it
When they see visions of banks and government's corruption
They gone brown paper bag their money with no hesitation
All we want is the conversation
A place at the table
Are you willing and able?
We want a plateau to speak our mind
And let you know our pains
Or else you'll keep getting these harshly out spoken rebel sayings
Take us in... Understand us... Listen to us... Respect us as yours
The blood of Civil Rights, from our vein pours
Come on, having the conversation is the least you could do
In conversing you can get past the bravado, the ego, and excuses
Try to deduce as Sherlock deduces
Do you have the patience?
To have a simple conversation

Thanks… I Think

Well you did free us
Thus
Thank you
But I'm not blinded in this poem
It wasn't for our best interest, but your own
You wanted to unite a nation and regain control
The South was over stepping their role
They also had common interests across the big blue
And if Confederates won, Britain would align away from
you
That connection would definitely end you
So I guess there's still a thank you to be said
But we kind of were forced to wed
I mean the great George Washington did own slaves
But those forefathers do deserve praise
…for making a great business choice
And freeing slaves but trapping their voice
I'm thanking you for freeing us from the lion's den
But not the lion as he wears a grin
A full slave, partially freed, and three-fifths a man
How tough is that poker hand?
However, I took it with a wink
So, thanks… I think

What's Changed?

They tell you we need to go back to our roots
    But yeah weren't we slaves then? (What's yo name boy?)
    How's that a win?

They'll say these kids are bad
    But aren't they the kids of your kids?
    I mean, you're not even using a good weave that's a wig
    Covering up your flaws

How did that bridge burn?
    How did my generation get so judged by grandparents?
    And just forgotten by parents

We are you in a new generation
    We're fighting through mental slavery and civil rights
    We just chose a different way to fight

The rules to the game haven't changed, survive
    They may have slowed physical crack, but not mental
    They're subjecting us to visuals and its all so gentle

50 years later not much has changed
    To keep us down they gave us green faces
    So now instead of knowledge we chase money in all the
wrong places

They used crack on our elders
They use money on us
They use false education on our youth
(Continued)

So what's changed?
False inspirations have me feeling like a clown... where's the joke?
Yeah we got a black President so I can feel some hope
But they're trying to get him to hang himself by stringing up his own rope
Our participation in his progress will be the hands removing it from his throat
I mean cops and neighborhood watch killing minorities
And getting away with it; we're not priorities
We're beaten
We're battered
Spit on
Lied to
However, we're not defeated
There is a small flicker flickering in the shadows
I see it in the chance to show my siblings how to be strong
And how you can thank God for one more breath when everything's going wrong
After a mistake is made you can't be a hypocrite
Practice what you preach, keep gettin' it
No one is perfect, but a man... a woman stands tall
They get up after a fall
So you can sit on your can and complain about it all
I'm a try and make a positive change to history's wall

Seeing Color

Hard for the next generation to see color
Whenever Jay Z is liked by a white mother
But racism is still hanging around
Like a man trying not to drown
How can this still be?
It's hard for my eyes to see
Not for my pops though
He's still in pain from stubbing his toe
On blatant racism in the work place
Maybe not hoses and dogs, but still in his face
But how?
From a distance it's kind of like Undercover Brother
But it's not a joke to Trayvon Martin's mother
Mean while, Miley Cyrus is still twerking
Does that mean change is lurking?
Or is that just ratchetness working?
Good or bad she's crossed over the color road
The old guard thinks that's too bold
But what can they say to a J. Cole
Whose skin is white and black?
He raps so they see him as all black
Old guys hanging on to old ways
Black and white, it goes both ways
Seeing no color is growing, but so is the resistance
So how do we measure the distance
Of how far we've come in America?
And seeing no color

America's Step Son

I won't let the skeletons in the Mississippi rot
As I go along I'm changing your plot
America tried to abort me
But I still got my degree
And I'm bringing others with me
They tried to crack me but I won't break
Trying to trick us with a 'snow day' but that wasn't my fate
Never been to jail
I'm surviving your hell
All the plans you made to hold me back
I'm busting through all that
No drugs, no guns, and still no funds
Splitting these bread crumbs, till my next blessing comes
The illegitimate son of America
They grabbed new land in hopes of a 'land of the free' replica
But I'm going to use your rules against you
Don't think racism still about, don't be a fool
Obama, a half white Negro; President…
That system burns doesn't it!
But we're claiming black and African, when we may be more mulatto
White owners made a lot of black babies, far as I know
Then again, be composed of more Negro the door they'll show
I won't let the dead from Civil Rights be in vain though
I'm done playing your game, so
The prodigal son returns

Running, by Raheem E. Stanfield

I bumped into a strange man the other day
Or, rather he bumped me
Trapped in my own thoughts
I wrote his off
Angrily yelling "Can't you see?!"
But it was me turning a blind eye
And deaf ear
to the cry of a man stuck on the run
As I tapped his shoulder
He turned and my tongue got twisted
 as the felines made away with it
His tears were arrows
Leading me along the story that his face told
His eyes reflected the world
And he, as did his tears, fell

He, running away from the world

Heavy wrinkles and liver spots on a man no older than 35
Told of a world of pain
I wondered why he was running away
And his face responded,
 an absent father,
 a dirty, junky mother,
 and the family responsibilities of 30 years
 bestowed upon a life of 16
Lonely
Feeling no one else felt his pain,
knew his walk of life
He began to run.
Watching his mother
(Continued)

He learned how to get his stride correct
Unable to secure suitable employment to provide
He ran more often,
He ran faster,
He ran harder
Living the dirty life his mother lived,
no one wanted to stop him,
give him refuge,
He kept running.

As his tears continued,
I saw that he wanted to stop running
The prospect of children
Made him yearn for the family walk of life
But an accidental abortion, miscarriage, and a still born later
He was a childless father
At odds with the world
He threw in the towel and ran
Trying to get as far away from his reality as possible
Soon he became a runner looking to escape the road
and follow Wylie Coyote on his descent
All he lives for is that short lived high
The moment when he can look down
After stepping off of the cliff…
…Running to Die

(Inspired by Gil Scott Heron's "Home Is Where the Hatred Is")

Troubles

You bring the pain healer, I'll bring the pain
Troubles of this world, hard to maintain
Hard to stay sane
Let alone stay the same
Maybe if I had *Mo Money* I could
But I've never saved as I should
A little 'me' running around
I gotta beat these troubles down
School loans and maintaining credit
Trying to buy my way to success with a debit
Will never work when I'm paying with change
And $20 is way outta range
Troubles of a young man not a statistic
But a black man so let's be realistic
Hard to stay idealistic
When you see between the lines
Our lanes are smaller and crossing causes fines
Waiting on us to crash and burn
It may be what we've earned
Reparations won't help when a shiny whip is all we yearn
Look at our overall financial actions
All that counts are our distractions
We just want to keep our grills clean, no crest
We wear a shiny cross on our chest
Instead of a vest
Three shots to the breast
God wants us to have strong faith and be smart
Not pretend a bullet is a dart
(Continued)

That can be brushed off
Troubles created for us
But perpetuated by us
The real Constitution
Man made pollution
Slowing us down, asthma in the race
We sniff it, smoke it, shoot it, and sip it
Dilated eyes and liquor breath, what's with it?
More in jail than in classes
Why do we keep taking these free passes?
The easy way out is freely given
We've got to work
Haven't we learned anything from the past?
Or are we just the same old show with a new cast?
I guess it's just the troubles of this world, growing fast

Home Sweet Home

Am I that special?
I mean, they built me a home
Three meals a day and a little space to roam
I can learn a trade
The books are already paid
Life, I got it made
They treat others like me just as good
But hey, I'd also spread wealth where I could
Got me a nice regiment
Before leaving my house I am hesitant
People still have evil intent
But what's different on the outside?
You may think I'm lost or my mind is fried
Man, I'm just home sweet home
I'll fight to keep it that way
And if I leave, I'll be back soon they say
Repeat offender
Home, sweet home

Lost Royalty

When did we lose our royalty?
Was it when we lost loyalty?
Was it when we regulated God to once a week?
When we shut Him up and began to speak?
When we gave into stereotyping and perception?
Or when we gave power to the deception?
When did we lose it?
When we were sold by our own to the ships on their voyage?
Or when we gave away our papas porridge?
Did we ever know we were Kings and Queens?
Did it ever creep into our realities out of our dreams?
Ahhh…
We never lost it, just forgot as we were boxed in
Well here's a reminder then
I now crown you Royalty!
The spirit I'm invokin'
Is lost royalty that needed to be awoken
Take in the power of our ancestors
Our royal predecessors
Rise like the phoenix burning all the lies
And fly to the skies
Bringing back to Earth the heart and soul of those who came
before
The ones who opened that door
When did we forget?
When did we give in?
When did we become weak?
When did we fall asleep?
You want royalty again?
…Well, time to wake up!

Pastime Paradise

Now-a-days we spend most our lives just living
The worst things are said and done, but we're just kidding
I'm not from the old days but I miss 'em
I wish I could see our ancestors, grasping their wisdom
Building pyramids and influencing culture and the world
Seeing what started my culture and how our influence unfurled
But we're not living in a pastime paradise
We're living depending on a roll of dice
We can, however, create a future paradise
A place where equal is really equal
The next generation has potential for a great sequel
Qualified people and great minds can equal currency
Not living lazy, but with a sense of urgency
Learn from the past to change our future for the better
All those years of slavery and segregation go into the shredder
Should we stop wallowing in ignorance like pigs in mud
We can kick ignorance and be free of that drug
We protect our young like a shield
And mold them like strong bricks to build
Then we're on our way to a future paradise
…now that would be nice

With a Vengeance

I rather die enormous than live dormant
I can't sit and wait, I'm attacking like a hornet
If I don't I'll be in this box forever
My plan isn't anything clever
I'm a get it however I can
That's the plan
What have I got to lose?
On our inner city news
The outside world hits snooze
I didn't arrive at this mind state out the blue
If you were driven here what would you do?
I have to get out; friends either dead or in jail
A hurricane doesn't scare me, I'm setting sail
A crowded project, waves are going to crash
No one has time or space to grow like the grass
You're left saying, "I was just with him yesterday"
That's just how it goes around my way
I'm not going to jail so I'm a make it
Or die trying to take it
That so called American Dream
I've been in this boxed jail my whole life
I don't have room to think twice
Hence this
I'm going after that American Dream with a vengeance
…no matter how brief it may be

No Title

We're killing ourselves stupid
Wanna be hard, gangsta, and ruthless
You got a problem with the 'white man' well you doing the job for
him
When you gone stop killing and save them?
Your people
Your equal
Your eventual sequel
There's no cultural growth in sight
The lack of, is dimming the light
Just quick rich; no longevity in our health
Our worth holds no wealth
All the positives are stealth
We're content shaking butts, ballin', and flashing cash
Getting high and drunk and 'white boy' smashed
Get past the color, where is the cultural love?
I'll wait...
It's all love till we feel threatened and our pride is hurt
Then back to that cultural killing machine we revert
These rappers got everyone thinking they're a boss even on the
curb
To be a leader you must first follow and serve
Jesus taught me that. Who's feet do you wash?
Or is that beneath you?
If the crab next to you is climbing will you push or pull?
Look in the mirror, what are you doing for your cultural?
For your God?
For your people?

Dreamin', By Maal G

We're at our deepest state
Not knowing in our hand that we're holding the fate/
Check out your mental state/
Notice the change around you case we just can't wait/
Notice the people around you if they just stay fake/
Know that the strong survive and the weak gone break/
Build up your real-estate
Dealing with no land then they destined to hate/
Sitting here thinking and it called a debate/
Seeing my people lose but it's not too late/
Wait, moving fast with no plan you at a standstill/
Move with a goal or the next man will/
Losing the opportunity you wanted to chill/
Thinking it was facade when you wanted the real/
Now instead of destroy you feel you ready to build/
Well the build your empire, spark the new fire, weave out the liars
and walk to new higher heights /
Be smart when you're picking a fight/
You never know when you're losing your life
And that's why, uh and that's why..../

Be a King

I'm a Kinggggg
Martin flowing through my soul
My soul is old
Jesus Christ in my veins
I carry the cross to share his pain
This is the life of Kings
Back when the sands were in command
When the reign of man was grand
Kings sat atop thrones built on blood, sweat, and tears
On the backs of slaves and their fears
A merciful king or a tyrant; where's the line drawn
Let's see how you move your pawns
Are you serving or self serving?
This is the life of Kings
And I'm a King
The blood of African nations empowering me
The voice of ancestors guiding me
Carrying on my Kingship by playing my role
In the footsteps of my parents who are my foundation
Looking for a Queen of non-royal creation
Treating her like there is no other worthier
I sought God first, so I see her worth
Her exceptional manor makes her the more desirable
This is the life of Kings
Being a man first
Who puts others first
Represent the ones before like they're still here
Celebrate them with cheer
With no crown, you're a King
Even if your story no one will ever sing
My Malibu serves as my chariot
Be a King

No Ceilings

I see none
Though America tries to give one
Oh, they'll tell you otherwise
But when you look to the skies
It's there; all the lies
Look at an angle and you'll see a glass reflection
There may be gaps in each section
That's where you concentrate and focus
But some say it's fake and hopeless
Killing dreams is their sole purpose in life
I challenge you not to think twice
It's a struggle, but see no ceilings
Nothing can stop me in my dream dealings
I'm looking to shake up this world
And be a myth rarely seen like the Black Pearl
Trying to erase the old rules
While looking like fools
Because of out dated tools
If we only realize the power in our Kings and Queens
There'll be no ceilings to our dreams

His Son

The father is passing on
All he has left is his son
Last moments, his life in a flash
Together memories clash
Was I a good father to my child?
Was I a hot head, or did I keep my wings mild?
Reflection time
Time time time
It passes so fast
Like a mad dash
Lord what to do?
1 Kings Chapter 2
Verse one through three
This is what God wanted the father to see
He said son if nothing else follow these words
They'll keep you on the path even when it curves
When it's all said and done
That verse could be the most important thing he gave his son

1 Kings 2:1-3 (NIV)
1) When the time drew near for David to die, he gave a charge to
Solomon his son. 2)"I am about to go the way of all the earth," he
said. "So be strong, show yourself a man, 3) and observe what the
LORD your God requires: Walk in his ways, and keep his decrees
and commands, his laws and requirements, as written in the Law of
Moses, so that you may prosper in all you do and wherever you
go,…"

Speaker

Sitting next to the speakers hearing the sounds
Some laughs and some screams, so more frowns
Gun shots ring out
Somebody just got laid out
Sirens ringing loud
Somebody was acting too proud
A mother cries
As her son says sorry and dies
I hear her scream all kinds of whys

Next to the speaker with my eyes closed
Feeling the heat from the sun that just rose
Kids laughing and playing
Hopefully from school they're not straying
Eww you got cooties
Says a girl to a boy who thinks she's a cutie
Puppy love so innocent
Yea I remember this
Then kids turn to young adults and its graduation
Natural maturation
Glad to see this group made it
I've heard many with a gift who betrayed it

Sitting down by the speaker with my pad and pen
Taking in all the sounds brought in by the wind
Listening for more positives then negatives
More people sticking together like relatives
But instead there is a lot of beef and foolishness
Craziness and added stress
So when it gets too tough for my ears to deal with
I just close the window to block it
My window speakers to the world

Take Me Away

I'm sitting on the bench
Waiting for my spaceship
But it has seemingly passed me by
Didn't even stop and say bye
I just want to be taken away
From the dog days
Hard days ahead
This area looks like a head just free of dreads
Empty spaces and a wreck
But I'm still waiting

I want to flee the hard ships and tribulations
The deaths and complications
It's a part of life but painful none the less
But for that person it's the best…
I can't get them out my mind
I feel them grabbing my spine
Lord take me away from this world of sin
This world out of control in a tail spin
But without a Baloo and Kid
With them, that's where the joy is
(Continued)

Take me away to the clouds
Where there are no crowds
Where my mother can be proud
Where I can see clearly now
Take me to the joy
Where again I can be a baby boy
Take me away from bad government
Horrible politics
From racism and stereotypes
From people beating each other with pipes
Just yet, I can't go to that place
So determination you see on my face
Big task to change the world as one person
Actions louder than words and I'm first in

Across the Lake

If heaven was across Lake Erie, I would go
I would load a small boat and go
Taking nothing with me
Just a compass to lead me
I would leave all the pains of this world behind
Leaving the hard work and steady grind
Finally finding what I was trying to find
I would miss my family and friends of course
But I would want to be with the Lord

If heaven was a mile across the lake?
In leaving would I cause more heartache?
Would that be doing the people who love me wrong?
Who decides right and wrong?
I would hope they understood my motivation
Take my eyes and see my observation

If heaven was across the way
Would you tell a widow who lost her only child to wait one more
day?
I'm not talking about suicide, but the comfort of the creator
If you had a boat would you tell them see ya later?
What about the man who has to live disabled?
Would you tell him that heaven is just a myth or a fable?

If heaven was just over the horizon would that tempt you?
Set out towards the yellow sun; around it reflections of blue
Seeing granddad again is so enticing
Like them fly kicks at sale pricing
Could I honestly pass up those shoes?
Ask this, could you?

Heaven is across the lake of your mind

Crying Tears

She begs and pleads
Threatens and leaves
But she always comes back because she wants a father for her
seeds
The life he lives has a low life expectancy
She's on him relentlessly
To be in their lives is more important than monetary gain
After he was slain
She cried tears for him

Her son is in danger every second of every day
It just is that way
He defends our rights
Way beyond our sights
He volunteered for that life
The only way he sees her now is through Skype
Big giant tears she begins to wipe
When decorated soldiers arrive at her door
For her son she cries tears galore

They weren't suppose to overcome stereotypes at 21 let alone 27
Flooded eyes of parents look to heaven
Thanking God
As their son and daughter walk that graduation isle
Tears flowing like downstream, though they're all smiles
There will still be struggles but this is a victory
For them the parents laid tears of joy over tears of misery

Talking Walls

If these walls could talk
They would start with the chalk
Outlining a dead kid with holes in his frame
The scene is surreal, but this isn't a game
And there's no restart after that
Stupid killings over stupid things, so whack
Colors, pride, who is hardest, who is the better rapper
It's really about who is the better actor
Thug class 101
Where did this come from?
"We" are creating this facsimile
That's being copied and distributed throughout the community
How do we turn these cons into pros?
Only the wall with Jesus' picture frame knows

If these walls could spill the beans
They would tell tales of crack heads and fiends
How greed over took my so called brothers
Crossing the line to take care of their mothers
Is it worth it in the end?
Leading to another's death is still a sin
And taking matters into your own hands won't get the win
Those walls have seen the young die fast
Done in by their supporting cast
Or so called friends
They're speeding down a slippery slope indeed
And that car gets tough to stop at that speed
(Continued)

If those walls could speak
They would tell of crooked policies and people that were weak
Old men with no knowledge of today
Still living in an old and out dated way
Looking for whoever can peak their interest or fatten their wallet
What's his name; senator, governor, or president what-cha-ma-call it?
Lobbyist waiting in large lobbies to lobby for themselves
Not the people they were chosen for, to change how they dwell
Rephrase...
Lobbyist waiting in large lobbies to lobby for their pimp
Instead of helping that old war vet living in the projects with a limp

If these here walls could talk
They would speak of a hard walk
Trusting in God it'll turn out fine
Just a brain in a voice box, speaking in my mind
But these walls are talking in the form of a pen
Lord forgive us all of our sin
The ones that go on in between physical walls
And the ones that gather with a voice in a tight area like bathroom stalls
A hole in the wall of my brain has been punctured and starts to leak...
This is how a wall speaks

Faceless

A faceless woman she has now become
This new lady I don't know where she came from
Everything that was right is now wrong
It's like someone changed the lyrics to our song
Crazy looks and mean mugs for breakfast
Sighs and silence for dinner before rest
No more movie nights
We have our own paper view fights
Trying to figure her out now is more complicated than before
I had her heart now it's behind a closed door
And she stays there locked away
It's a struggle, in our own house seeing her every other day
The answer to the cause I'm still searching
The answer is out there, lurking
Is someone else taking up her time?
Is there someone else on her mind?
I rarely see that smile she used to display
Now between us is a large area of grey
Large area of empty space
So I stare at the area that should be her face
Faceless and no emotion in her eyes
So is she looking at me or other guys?

Shadow

Walking in the darkness I am
But it's not my fault I am
I'm going the extra mile for her
Because I love her
But walking in the dark the shadow consumes
On and off our relationship resumes
She can't get past the past
And I want her to fast
Her past is blocking a bright future
Like the sun behind clouds hiding the beauty of her
In the dark we hold battles
I wish she would leave these shadows
For the light of us

Double Dare

She said
"Let me be your one and only
This is no joke, no phony
I'm worthy of the task at hand
I complete the band
I can save you from whatever scar is ripping through your
heart
I can mend that part
When we hug, we stare, we talk its real
Can we be real?
Just because you love someone doesn't mean you'll be
But give me that chance and we'll see
As difficult as giving your heart can seem
Once you take that step it's like a dream
I dare you…
I double dare you…"

Crossing the Line

He spent so much time and energy trying not to cross the line
But there's always that one time
Flood gates open
What it became it was never suppose to be
And he apologizes to she
Sometimes you get caught up in the moment
Happens to everyone, hopefully they'll find some atonement
He spent the same amount of time trying to get back to the safe
side of the line
The chill of his mistake rides up his spine
Poetry is his time machine
It allows him to return to the past and erase the sting
That line he crossed got blurred upon crossing
So it got hard to find again even while slowly walking
…right over it
Will he ever get over it?
What's done is done, the line was crossed over
And now a new line is created and must be watched over

Why Chase

Why chase love when you're not ready?

A platonic relationship with no strings usually grows them like vines
Expectations start getting ticketed and come with fines
The random fun becomes expected time together
What was so great is starting to sever
She's ready. He's not
She slowly stepped to the spot
Don't run to the kitchen if it's hot
But he gave chase. She indulged
In her chest she felt a bulge
A feeling
She ignored and played along
Now everything is wrong

Why chase love when you're not ready?

The expectations hit and he explains his stance
She returns with an evil glance
Feelings get hurt
Everything that did, doesn't work
He's reluctantly giving chase to love, but he's not ready
He may look it in the face, but he's far from steady
It hurts every time he loses
Leaves unseen bruises
Why does he put himself through it?
Why does she put herself through it?
Why do they do it?
Why do they chase love?

The Game We Play

Make up to break up, that old song and dance
But somehow it's got us in a trance
An unsturdy stance
So now I got a new girl, you got a new dude
But we can't give up what we had, how rude
So the lies start to cover up our time together
We're creating stormy weather
It seems we're better in separate relationships
Only causing hardships
But we can't see it in the moment
Our mates do and they can't take it, but then again who could
Now we're blaming each other for not being able to walk away
Trying to hold on to them knowing it wouldn't work anyway
Now we're back together in that 'I missed you' stage
Look up and here come the clouds; situations creating rage
Last time it was a male friend of yours
Now it's a female friend of mine that's bringing the heat out your pours
I knew I shouldn't have read her that poem when she asked
But I was feeling a little gassed
Built without truth this will never last
Same 'ol show, but we're the only returning cast
Make up to break up, that old song and dance
But somehow it's got us in a trance
An unsturdy stance
The game we play

When She Says Come Back

Maybe we can try this again is what she said to me
But I thought we'd never again be
Not that we couldn't
Just we wouldn't
Both moving forward, to go back just seems…
Some things are just better let go
But what if this is the 'come back' part
There's no way to dodge that dart
It's hard to pick up right before where we left off
Right where we left off was the grey cloud
But before there was none found
There were short spurts of rain and long intervals of
sunshine
I hear her whisper in my ear with her hand on my spine…
"Come back"

I Wish

Sometimes I wish I didn't love you
Take my eyes and see my view
It would make things simple
It would hide that pimple
That I know you see
And you can tell what it's doing to me
But "love" conquers all
But our love is leading to a big fall
If I didn't love you I could just walk away
I wouldn't have to say it each day
But I do love you and that's why this is hard to say
It's hard to tell you that we've run our course
We're an empty water source
We see things differently and there's no need to force the issue
If you need 'em I got a box of tissue
Every time I build the nerve
She resets serve
It's always 40 love and she comes back
How do I stop that?
I don't want to but I see the full photograph
And you're in this half and half
So I'm sorry boo
This is a time I wish I didn't love you

Most Addictive in the World

I got a taste of it, now I want more
I wasn't before, but now I'm sure
There is nothing more addicting than this
So priceless it's sealed with a kiss
If you don't have, for it you'll wish
It got me up all hours of the night
With no glasses got me staring into the light
It has me willing to jump off a building
For this there is no healing
Most addictive drug created can't come close
It embodies its host
Gives joy and pain all at one time
Hope to get it in your prime
What has me feeling this you ask?
…that thing called love…

She Don't Know, Won't Hurt Her

What she don't know won't hurt her
So I move like a steady blur
In and out of her sight
But being ever so polite
I tell her I love her and I'll be back
And I really mean that
I mean both
The love is readl, she's my forever

But what she don't know won't hurt her

Came in late from a playa move
Trying to be quiet, smooth
But she's awake, tears in her eyes
Bruise on her arm huge in size
Real concern on my face and in my voice
She doesn't know where it came from or how
I just think she's embarrassed about her clumsy style
To the bedroom she goes
I check my phone to see a thick chicks pose
Noise in the bathroom, she's in pain
Another bruise and now this is racking my brain
Is she sensitive to touch?
Her skin can't take a soft brush?
(Continued)

I thought what she didn't know wouldn't hurt her

Late to dinner, by now you know why
Feeling high as the sky
But I can see something in her eye
Sweat down my back
Does she know the facts?
Nah, it can't be that
There's another bruise on her
As I start to think
The events in my mind start to link
The bruises have a real correspondence
I thought it wouldn't hurt…
But I guess it's really true…
"It's ironic, if I hit another chick its gone bruise you"*

*quote by J. Cole

If I'm Special

She said if I'm special
Why aren't you more careful?
Like that golf handicap why aren't you more helpful?
If I'm special, why don't you treat me so?
Why do you block my glow?
If I'm so special
Why are things so stressful?
If I'm special why don't I feel it?
Like a horse and a whip
Like the waves throwing a ship
You say I'm special so why do you need a script to act?
It should come easier than that
If I'm your special one
Why can't I be the Earth to your sun?
Spinning in a dance with you till we're done
If I'm so special, why can't we last forever?
Like eternal life as God's gift to treasure
She said if I'm so special why do you treat me this way?
After all that, I had nothing to say

Not Coming Back

"You're gonna want me back"

The old saying is true
Never miss a good thing till it's gone
Man I did her wrong
I beat the crap out of her without ever laying a finger
I mentally hit her with the Tiger stinger
A low strategic shot staying under the wind
My actions were a slap in the face; a right cross to the chin
Instead of being on my hands and knees mopping up her tears
I was pool side oblivious to them killing her fears
Because once she doesn't fear losing me
She's free to leave me
One more knock on the chin
She got up right before the count of ten
Man she gave me chance after chance to step up
Now she's running like makeup
In the opposite direction of me
Took a week for me to break down
For me to aimlessly drive around town
For me to lose purpose
And what's worse
I really loved her and knew she loved me
I had to really mess up for her not to come back
But why would she come back?
She ain't coming back

2 Men

I was at a table in the presence of two men
There they told me to take a stand
Defend all my actions and choices
Did I do right and follow the right voices
Did I follow the morals and values handed down to me
Did I do things ethically?
How did I choose my friends?
In the deal did I hold up my end?
Did I follow the crowd or create my own lane
When it was going down did I stay on the plane?
Did I let go what wasn't good for me
Did I pass up personality for pretty?
Personality over pretty and patience over haste
Cause when you're face down you can't see a pretty face
Did I show that patience in key moments?
Or was I the one blowing it
These two men tried to tare me down
But I wouldn't frown
I was built from the ground up, strong
And I take total responsibility for being wrong
I tried to keep my heart in play
And let it lead my way
The heart stands out more than plastic surgery
And taking time for real love is better than love perjury
(Continued)

Did I, did I, or didn't I
Why didn't I ask them why?
Why didn't I give them a shoulder to cry?
Why didn't I give her another chance?
Did I leave it in God's hands?
Right at my strongest I was feeling a little weak
Like at the end of a winning streak
I thought deep but not that deep
Over dosing on regret I was on the verge
Timed passed and the two men began to merge
Clearing up the lines that were blurred
And seeing my face in the mirror

My Friend JD

When I'm around you I feel at home
When I'm with you I feel I'm atop my throne
I'll always love you
There's no me without you
You're like a brother to me
When I'm down you make me believe I can do anything
You're Maverick on my wing
And because of that there's jealousy
When we part we return with expediency
I trust no one more than you
And the advice you give is never false, always true
Without you in my corner what would I do?
I would have to go to rehab to get rid of this feeling
For that I am not willing
You know him as Jack Daniels
But to me he's just JD

Raft

It's just them and the nights glow
The catamaran is in tow
They're too weak to row
The struggle is real
Whatever hand the dealer deals
Diamond in the onion but first are the tears
He keeps telling her
That big break will occur
Soon
She's losing faith
Like a follower of pastor Mase
Who sees him rapping
What's happening?
They were riding the waves like the best surfer
Now at every turn he hurts her
The waves are choppy and the winds are high
He doesn't want to let his dream die
Or lose his dream girl; he looks to the sky
His tears disappear into the ocean
The fairytale potion
Is fading
His confidence is degrading
He's just trying to keep them afloat
On the raft

Crossing the Mississippi

Struggling a bit here
It's not due to fear
But it's tough to follow dreams when a strange current is pulling
I see clearly the path needed
I see the warning signs being heeded
No one ever said it would be easy to reach the other side
For their own dreams many have died
If I believe in myself as others do then I have no reason not to cross
Every situation isn't going to have that shiny gloss
Not everyone can afford the cost
The cost of either succeeding or failing
The water is cold and the wind is wailing
But once I take that first step and dive in I hit rock bottom
Literally
But sometimes there's a fall before a rise
The Red Sea parts and I'm walking on solid ground
Even a little bit of faith will help you not to drown
Dust myself off and head in the direction of my dreams thanking
God all the way
I now see my so called problems from a different angle and view
It may not be done the same way for you
But you can cross the Mississippi too

Fight of the Salmon

Born to die, struggling to live
All the life it has, it gives
The ultimate sacrifice by one
The journey they'd die for to get done
An upstream battle all the way
But the drive to fight every day
Knowing the outcome of the fight changes nothing
This is their ultimate something
To find your purpose in life and not fight it
Respect it, can't deny it
To hear and follow God's plan without question
Will you submit like Charleston Heston?
AKA Moses
We, like the salmon know it's going to end
What struggle and ultimate sacrifice are you overcoming
until then?

Grey

They looked at them twice, like they were an attractive couple
But it slowly dawned on him; it was because they were a couple
We have come a long way but there is more territory to travel
More boundaries to knock down and unravel
Some people were just raised that way
But today is a new day
That old way of thinking is just about dead
Get that color barrier out cha head
It's beautiful like a black car with white interior
Just because you're one color doesn't make you inferior
Privilege is given by men and hate is taught
And freedom in no way should have to be bought
Without titles everyone is equal
And these petty differences are just that, feeble
So as people look at them funny
It's them who play the dummy
If you must give them a color, you must think that way…
No black or white; they're just grey

Changing the World

I heard you can't change the world until you change yourself
That change equals wealth
So you start with the man in the mirror and the rest will follow
That dream is very far from hollow
But how can one person change the world?
Well you change you and you show love to one person, it can
change their world
You can't change all if you don't start with one
Not all will follow and changing bad habits will be a challenge
There always has to be balance
For all the evil there's just as much good, probably more
It's a simple change like the beach shore
The tide coming up and reshaping the sands
The choice is in your hands
If you wanna make the world a better place
Look at yourself and make a change

Shout Out to Obama

President Obama is a great step, but not the end all
The King dream can still stall
And that's the worst fall
It's like he got in office and we've become satisfied
We hid behind the first black President and the dream no longer applied
Don't waste the tears cried
The blood shed
The ones dead
That step made us 7 feet tall but with Z* hops
Mean while Blake Griffin is flying high with no stops
Let's not let him be a charity to shut us up

Shout out to the President
We know it isn't all equal
This movie is just another prequel
Another leader of black shade being undermined
While they're sitting across the table from him being wined and dined
All of a sudden the seat of the President isn't all that
Oh is that a fact?
Did we forget about Bush?
We didn't but they did
One of the worst Presidents to ever live
An uphill battle is being fought and it seems he's alone

Shout out to President Obama for fighting a losing fight
He sees America through different sight
Call him naïve for thinking we can be Americans and come together
For thinking we can look past sides and get past the oncoming weather
Even if it brings this country down
Some will not come around
If no one else will support him beyond policy I will
Shout out to My President

- Pre second term
- *Zydrunas Ilgauskas

Give Thanks

Thanksgiving isn't about Pilgrims and Native Americans alone
To me it's about all Americans that roam
We can't change the past, but our future is a different story
We can have a better future giving God glory
Thanksgiving is about good friends and family
Giving God thanks for the blessings He's given me
The tough times He's pulled me through, I say thanks
This is just a thank you letter with the name blank
You fill it in and tell all the people you love thanks
Tell the people that love you thanks
Tell God thanks
Even tell the "haters" thanks
God puts people and situations in your life for a reason
So know that it's more to the season
Give thanks

Thank You's

God, I struggle still
Jorden, you humble me. I understand true love and sacrifice
Mom and Dad
Raheem, Demetria and Tommie Lee (I'm proud of y'all. Congrats on the graduation Rah)
My Grandparents (Tommie Sr., Christine)
Momma C

My Uncles, Aunts, and Cousins; I love and appreciate all of you!

My Friends; I respect y'all and appreciate the inspiration and support.

Dev, Rah, Maal G; thanks for the contributions!

Thanks to all my Twitter, IG, and Facebook friends!

My cousin Charles, thanks for the visuals!

My cousin J Rawls, I was humbled to be in your studio. Much appreciation.

Rat Pack, What Up!

Lulu.com

Thank You!

Tears for My Princess

Looking at this world I'm apart of crying tears
Tears of affirmed fears
Crying true tears of fears for my daughter
This world leads its lambs to the slaughter
House
With a yellow wolf ready to pounce
Preparing to retain wise words for her I lose thoughts
All I can recall are my faults
And I guess she can learn from that
Man, it's harder than pulling a rabbit out a hat
I just want her to uphold morals and values
Have a third eye ready for these foul dudes
I want her to know she's not alone
She has aunts and uncles to phone
She has a mother whose love for her is unmeasured
A bond and a love never to be severed
As much as I want to protect her
I can't contain her
I pray I can give her the tools to make good choices
And listen to God above all the other voices
(Continue)

I hope to be as wise and handy as my pops
As calm and sincere as my uncle Al, props
Tears are drying as I think of my family
They'll always stand by me
And therefore by my princess
Even when it seems senseless
In distress or sickness
I want her to have a love for all her family as I
I can't control, I can only prepare a path
And then it's up to her to do the math
For a reason I guess a parent only understands
From my eyes are tears for my baby girl

Welcome to the Struggle

Welcome to the struggle
Where gun shots are loud but death is muffle
1 in 5 gets reported, but you heard about that dog in the
sewer right?
What about that mother, who's to sooth her through the
night?

Welcome to the struggle
Where they just broke up and her heart is open again
All the love is flowing out and in need of a manhole to stop
the drain
Pain and hate are creeping in her brain
She struggle to keep from going insane
He said he didn't have to call her beautiful because she has
plenty saying so
But to her it matters more who is saying so
It should've been him

Welcome to the struggle
Where pops just got denied for the third time
They don't like guys who've done time
And time is of the essence, he has a family to provide for
Hopefully the next time will be the right time and open up
that door
(Continued)

Welcome to the struggle
Where I couldn't afford her love so I bought it using my
credit card gaining triple interest
So I lost it all when she lost interest
The struggle between being a sucker for love and a slave to
fighting off the feeling
Fighting off the healing
And falling in love with the pain
Maybe you can figure out the gain?

Welcome to the struggle
Where we can become the masters of our fate
If we have faith salvation will not be denied us, whatever
the world's state
Life was never promised easy
But you climb that mountain and things get breezy
Its gonna be a struggle but make sure your grip is tight
And continue to fight
You're not alone

Welcome to the struggle

"During my lifetime I have dedicated myself to this struggle of the African people. I have fought against white domination, and I have fought against black domination. I have cherished the ideal of a democratic and free society in which all persons live together in harmony and with equal opportunities. It is an ideal which I hope to live for and to achieve. But if needs be, it is an ideal for which I am prepared to die."

– Nelson Mandela

"Progress is not just handed down as a gift, it is won through struggle - the struggle of men and women who believe things can be better, who refuse to accept the world as it is but dream of what it can be. Nelson Mandela was the embodiment of that struggle."

– UK Prime Minister David Cameron

R.I.P. Nelson Mandela

www.ingramcontent.com/pod-product-compliance
Lightning Source LLC
Chambersburg PA
CBHW020909090426
42736CB00008B/550